Wine Tasting Words

Quick Guide

Learn quickly what 'foxy, buttery, elegant, velvety, cat pee, baked...' and more means in the world of wine lovers.

3rd Edition published by Guts-Ad, LLC
Copyright © 2013-2017 by Guts-Ad, LLC

Wine Tasting Words
by MyWineShirt

ISBN-13: 978-0615941523 (Guts-Ad, LLC)
ISBN-10: 0615941524

Visit our websites:
www.Guts-Ad.com/Wine

Follow us on twitter:
@MyWineShirt

"EVERYBODY HAS A DIFFERENT TASTE. FIND YOUR OWN FAVORITE WINE."

MyWineShirt

"THERE IS NO ABSOLUTE RIGHT OR WRONG WHEN IT COMES TO WINE TASTES."

MyWineShirt

WINE TASTING WORDS:

Taste Collection

PEAR *drop*

FRUIT *— forward —*

Pétillant

Tannin

VELVETY

— fine — BUBBLES

— burned — TOAST

fairly mature

ELEGANT

flabby

Piquant

Brilliant

LICORICE

POWERFUL

ACID: IT IS A SHARP, TART EFFECT OF THE GREEN FRUIT OF YOUNG WINE ON BOTH THE NOSE AND TONGUE.

Acid

ASTRINGENT: IT IS THE ROUGH TASTE CAUSED BY AN EXCESS OF TANNIN. YOU WILL FIND THIS ESPECIALLY IN YOUNG RED WINES. THIS TASTE DECREASES WITH AGE IN THE BOTTLE.

Astringent

BAKED: THIS APPLIES TO WINES OF HIGH ALCOHOLIC CONTENT. IT IS TYPICALLY FOR GRAPES HARVESTED IN GREAT HEAT–EITHER FROM A HOT COUNTRY OR FROM A CLASSIC WINE AREA IN A HOT YEAR. THIS CHARACTERISTIC CAN BE CONTROLLED TO SOME EXTENT BY METHODS LIKE EARLY HARVESTING AND NIGHT HARVESTING.

Baked

Taste Collection

BALANCED: A WINE WITH ALL ITS COMPONENTS IN HARMONY. NO ELEMENT (MAINLY ACIDITY, ALCOHOL, FRUIT, TANNINS, SUGAR, AND EXTRACT) SHOULD BE PROMINENT.

Balanced

BOUQUET: THIS SHOULD REALLY BE APPLIED TO THE COMBINATION OF SMELLS DIRECTLY ATTRIBUTED TO A WINE'S MATURITY IN BOTTLE. USE THE WORD "AROMA" FOR GRAPE-RELATED SMELLS AND "BOUQUET" FOR MATURATION-RELATED SMELLS. HOWEVER, IT IS NOT ALWAYS POSSIBLE TO USE THESE WORDS IN THEIR PUREST FORM, WHICH IS WHY AROMA AND BOUQUET MAY BE CONSIDERED SYNONYMOUS.

Bouquet

BREED: WINE HAS THE TYPE, CHARACTER AND QUALITIES OF ITS ORIGIN.

BREED

BRILLIANT: LOOK AT THE WINE. IS IT BRIGHT AND SPARKLING IN APPEARANCE SO THAT ONE CAN SEE THE LIGHT THROUGH THE WINE? CALL IT BRILLIANT. IT IS THE OPPOSITE OF DULL AND CLOUDY.

Brilliant

BURNT RUBBER: THIS EFFECT COULD INDICATE A WINE FAULT CAUSED BY EXCESSIVE SULPHUR. HOWEVER IT IS WIDELY AND POSITIVELY ASSOCIATED WITH THE SYRAH GRAPE VARIETY.

burnt
RUBBER

BURNT TOAST: THIS IS THE RESULT OF USING OLD, CHARRED OAK BARRELS. THE RESULTING FLAVORS, MOST NOTICEABLY THE TASTE OF BURNT TOAST, CUT THE ACIDS IN THE WINE AS IT AGES.

FUN FACT: ANCIENT ROMANS LIKED TO PUT ACTUAL BURNT TOAST IN THEIR WINE CUPS TO ACCOMPLISH THE SAME THING. SOME PEOPLE SAY IT IS THE ORIGIN OF "TOASTING."

burnt

TOAST

Taste Collection

BUTTERY: THIS IS NORMALLY A RICH, FAT AND POSITIVELY DELICIOUS CHARACTER FOUND IN WHITE WINES. YOU CAN TASTE THIS FLAVOUR PARTICULARLY WHEN THE WINE HAS UNDERGONE MALOLACTIC FERMENTATION.

BUTTERY

CAT PEE: "THIOLS" ARE THE VOLATILE, SULPHUR-CONTAINING MOLECULES THAT GIVE SAUVIGNON BLANC ITS DISTINCTIVE SMELL. AT LOW LEVELS, THIOLS GIVE THE WINE ITS CHARACTERISTIC GOOSEBERRY, TROPICAL AND PASSIONFRUIT AROMA. HOWEVER AT HIGH LEVELS THEY CAN MAKE THE WINE SMELL LIKE CAT'S URINE.

Cat Pee

Taste Collection

CHARACTER: A WINE WITH TOP-GRADE DISTINGUISHING QUALITIES.

CHARACTER

CORKY: THE WINE HAS A DISAGREEABLE SMELL AND A FLAT TASTE OF ROTTEN CORK DUE TO A DEFECTIVE CORK IN THE BOTTLE.

CORKY

CRISP: THE WINE HAS A PLEASING SENSE OF ACIDITY.

crisp

Taste Collection

DRY: THE WINE IS COMPLETELY LACKING SWEETNESS. DO NOT CONFUSE IT WITH SOURNESS OR BITTERNESS.

DRY

EARTHY: A SOIL-LIKE AROMA COMMONLY IDENTIFIED IN OLDER BOTTLES OF RED BORDEAUX.

EARTHY

ELEGANT: USE THIS TERM TO DESCRIBE A GOOD-QUALITY AND BALANCED WINE THAT IS NOT TOO FRUITY. "AN ELEGANT WINE IS EXTREMELY PLEASANT TO DRINK."

ELEGANT

FAIRLY MATURE: A WINE THAT HAS AGED TO ITS PEAK POINT OF QUALITY.

fairly mature

FINE BUBBLES: THESE ARE PINPOINT AND VERY SMALL BUBBLES FROM A FINE CHAMPAGNE, WHOSE EFFERVESCENCE IS DUE TO FERMENTATION.

fine BUBBLES

FINESSE: USE THIS WORD TO DESCRIBE A WINE OF HIGH QUALITY THAT IS WELL BALANCED.

FINESSE

FINISH: THE TASTE THAT THE WINE LEAVES AT THE END, EITHER PLEASANT OR UNPLEASANT.

Finish

FLABBY: THIS IS THE OPPOSITE OF CRISP, REFERRING TO A WINE LACKING IN ACIDITY, AND CONSEQUENTLY DULL, WEAK, AND SHORT.

flabby

Taste Collection

FOXY: FEATURING THE SAME SMELL AS GRAPE JELLY, THIS IS A FLAVOR FOUND IN WINES MADE FROM NATIVE AMERICAN GRAPES, SUCH AS ZINFANDEL.

FOXY

FRUIT FORWARD: SOMETIMES WHEN YOU TASTE A WINE, ITS FRUITINESS JUMPS RIGHT OUT AT YOU. WINE LOVERS DESCRIBE SUCH WINES AS "FRUIT FORWARD." WINES FROM THE NEW WORLD– ESPECIALLY FROM THE UNITED STATES, AUSTRALIA, AND NEW ZEALAND–TEND TO BE MORE FRUIT FORWARD THAN EUROPEAN WINES, WHICH ARE CONSIDERED OLD WORLD.

FRUIT

forward

FRUITY: A WINE THAT HAS PLENTY OF ATTRACTIVE FRUIT FLAVORS.

Fruity

GRAPY: HAVING THE TASTE OR AROMA OF FRESH GRAPES, SUCH AS THE MUSCAT.

GRAPY

GREEN: THIS MEANS THE WINE IS HARSH AND UNRIPE WITH AN UNBALANCED ACIDITY, WHICH CAUSES A DISAGREEABLE ODOR AND A RAW TASTE.

Green

INSIPID: IN SHORT, DULL. WINE IS LACKING IN CHARACTER AND ACIDITY.

INSIPID

INTENSE FLAVORS: THIS DESCRIBES A WINE WHICH PACKS A PUNCH, FLAVOR-WISE. AN INTENSE WINE MAKES A BIG IMPACT ON YOUR PALATE. THIS DOESN'T MEAN THAT THE WINE IS NECESSARILY FULL-BODIED OR HEAVY. INSTEAD IT MEANS THAT IT HAS POWERFUL FLAVORS AND OFTEN HAS ACIDITY THAT HELPS MAKE THOSE FLAVORS STAND OUT.

INTENSE F FLAVORS

Taste Collection

JAMMY: COMMONLY USED TO DESCRIBE A FAT AND EMINENTLY DRINKABLE RED WINE RICH IN FRUIT, IF PERHAPS LACKING A BIT OF ELEGANCE.

jammy

LICORICE: THIS WINE HAS A HINT OF LICORICE. A QUALITY OFTEN DETECTED IN MONBA-ZILLAC, BUT MANY FOUND IN ANY RICH SWEET WINE. THE TERM REFERS TO THE CONCENTRATION OF FLAVORS FROM HEAT-SHRIVELED, RATHER THAN BOTRYTIZED GRAPES.

LICORICE

MADERIZED: THIS TASTING WORD IS APPLIED TO WINES THAT HAVE PASSED THEIR PRIME AND HAVE ACQUIRED A BROWN COLOR. THE WINE HAS A FLAT, OXIDIZED SMELL AND ITS TASTE REMINISCENT OF MADEIRA.

Maderized

MUSTY: WINE SMELLS AND TASTES MOLDY. IT HAS A DISAGREEABLE ODOR AND STALE FLAVOR CAUSED BY STORAGE IN DIRTY CASKS OF CELLARS.

MUSTY

Taste Collection

NOBLE: SUPERIOR AND DISTINGUISHED; NOT ONLY POSSESSING THE RIGHT CREDENTIALS BUT ALSO HAVING AN IMPRESSIVE STATURE OF ITS OWN.

NOBLE

PEAR DROP: IT'S THE TASTE OF A HARD CANDY, WHICH IS POPULAR IN ENGLAND. IT GETS FLAVORS FROM AN ESTER CALLED ISOAMYL ACETATE. IF THERE IS TOO MUCH ISOAMYL ACETATE IN A WINE, IT STARTS TO TAKE ON NEGATIVE AROMA, SUCH AS NAIL-POLISH.

PEAR drop

PEPPERY: THIS IS THE AROMATIC SMELL OF CERTAIN YOUNG RED WINES FROM HOT CLIMATES, AND IS COMMONLY ASSOCIATED WITH THE RED WINES OF SOUTHERN FRANCE (ESPECIALLY FROM THE RHONE VALLEY AND THE GRENACHE GRAPE VARIETY).

Peppery

PÉTILLANT: SIZZLING WITH AN NATURAL LIGHT SPARKLE, THIS IS THE FRENCH WORD FOR "SPARKLING."

Pétillant

PIQUANT: THE WINE IS PRICKLING YOUR PALATE WITH ITS TARTNESS, WHICH COMES FROM A DRY AND CRISPY ACID.

Piquant

POWERFUL: A "BIG" WINE WITH HIGH LEVELS OF EXTRACT AND/OR ALCOHOL. THIS TASTING WORD CAN BE USED IN A POSITIVE OR NEGATIVE SENSE.

POWERFUL

RED FRUIT: USE THIS WORD WHEN YOU TASTE FRUITS SUCH AS CHERRY, RASPBERRY, STRAWBERRY, CRANBERRY AND THE LIKE IN THE WINE.

red fruit

RICH FLAVORED: THE WINE IS CONCENTRATED, IMPLYING DEEP AND INTENSE FLAVORS IN THE MOUTH. IT CAN ALSO BE USED TO MEAN SLIGHTLY SWEET.

RICH
flavored

RIPE: WINE MADE FROM RIPE GRAPES AND SHOWING FLAVORS OF RICHER, WARMER-CLIMATE FRUITS, SUCH AS PINEAPPLES (RATHER THAN APPLES). RIPE WINE MIGHT ALSO SUGGEST A CERTAIN SWEETNESS, EVEN THOUGH IT MAY NOT CONTAIN SUGAR.

RIPE

SÉVE: IT IS THE CONCENTRATED AROMATIC TASTE OF A RIPE SWEET WHITE WINE OF INHERENT QUALITY. THIS IS THE SAP OF A GREAT WINE.

Séve

SMOKY: EASY TO DETECT, THE WINE HAS A SMOKY BOUQUET. IT IS A PARTICULAR BOUQUET OF CERTAIN LOIRE WINE, SUCH AS POUILLY-FUMÉ, MADE FROM THE SAUVIGNON GRAPE.

Smoky

Taste Collection

SMOOTH: TYPICALLY REFERS TO A WINE WITH SOFT TANNINS. USE THIS WORD TO DESCRIBE A WINE WITH A PLEASING TEXTURE.

SMOOTH

SPICY: THE AROMA IS RICHER AND MORE PRONOUNCED THAN WHAT WE CALL "FRUITY." IT IS THE DEFINITE AROMA AND FLAVOR OF SPICE ARISING FROM CERTAIN GRAPE VARIETIES, LIKE GEWÜRZTRAMINER.

SPICY

SULPHURY: REMINISCENT OF ROTTEN EGGS, IF THE SMELL DOES NOT DISAPPEAR AFTER THE WINE IS POURED, IT IS AN INDICATION THAT THE WINE IS FAULTY.

SULPHURY

SWEET: WINE HAS A HIGH CONTENT OF RESIDUAL SUGAR EITHER FROM THE GRAPE ITSELF OR AS THE PRODUCT OF ARRESTED FERMENTATION.

Sweet

Taste Collection

TANNIN: MOST PROMINENT IN RED WINE, A MAJOR COMPONENT IN THE STRUCTURE OF RED WINES. IT IS ALSO A NATURAL COMPONENT FOUND TO VARYING DEGREES IN THE SKINS, SEEDS AND STEMS OF GRAPES.

Tannin

TART: THIS WORD REFERS TO A NOTICEABLE ACIDITY SOMEWHERE BETWEEN PIQUANT AND SHARP.

TART

VELVETY: A WINE THAT WILL LEAVE NO ACIDITY ON THE PALATE. USE THIS WORD FOR A MELLOW RED WINE WITH A SMOOTH, SILKY TEXTURE.

VELVETY

VIGOROUS: USE THIS WORD FOR A WINE WHICH IS LIVELY, FIRM, YOUTHFUL. IT IS THE OPPOSITE OF INSIPID AND FLABBY.

VIGOROUS

WATERY: THIS WINE HAS NO BODY OR CHARACTER, AND IT TASTES THIN AND SMALL.

Watery

YEASTY: IT IS LIKE THE SMELL OF YEAST IN FRESH BREAD. IT HAPPENS WHEN THE WINE IS UNDERGOING A SECOND FERMENTATION, POSSIBLY BECAUSE IT WAS BOTTLED TOO EARLY, WHICH MEANS THE WINE IS FAULTY.

Yeasty

ZESTY: THIS TASTE IS NORMALLY FOUND IN CRISP, REFRESHING DRY WHITE WINES. YOU WILL FIND AROMAS OF LEMON, LIME AND SOMETIMES EVEN ORANGE.

ZESTY

5 STEPS TO ENJOY YOUR WINE TASTING

When you are at a wine tasting you should have fun.
And there are 5 simple steps to go through a tasting.

1. PICK UP THE GLASS

Pick up the glass and tilt it away from you
so you can check the color.

RED WINE:
Do you see purple, ruby, garnet, or red brick color?

WHITE WINE:
Do you see pale, straw-like, light green, golden,
amber or brown color?

Don't worry about the meaning yet...you will
know it after you taste the wine.

2. SWIRL THE GLASS A BIT

Swirl the glass a bit, which will release more of the natural aroma. The aroma is essential for every wine taste.

3. SMELL THE WINE

3/4 of what we can taste is due to the sense of smell. Smelling wine: Stick your nose down into the glass, move your head in a cross way and do a short sniffs – yes, like a dog! Do you smell oak, berry, flowers, vanilla or citrus? Simply say what you smell.

4. TASTE THE WINE

To taste the wine, swish it around your mouth. Your tongue has many taste buds at the front and back and sides, which give you the tastes sour, bitter, sweet and so forth. Think about what the wine tastes like:

A. You might taste the alcohol content, tannin level, acidity, sweet or dry.

B. You can taste the things like fruit, spice, woody, smokiness with reds. With white wines you might taste apple, pear, tropical or citrus fruits, honey, floral.

C. What is the aftertaste? Was it a long or short finish, full bodied or light bodied?

5. TELL YOUR FRIENDS

Wine is something that should be celebrated and shared with friends. The more often you do a wine tasting, think of the wine you taste and share your thoughts with other wine lovers–the taste, the smell the sight. By sharing and learning from each other, you will see, smell and taste the difference over time.

But always remember, everybody will have a different favorite wine. There is no absolute right or wrong when it comes to wine tastes, which is all part of the experience and pleasure of wine.

Enjoy.

MY WINE SHIRT™

WEAR A WINE TASTE ON A T-SHIRT.

All wine tastes are available on a t-shirt.

Shop for printed t-shirts at:
www.Guts-Ad.com/Wine

Licorice	Musty	Noble	Pear Drop	Cat Pee	Character

Brilliant	Burnt Rubber	Burnt Toast	Buttery	Fruity	Grapy

Earthy	Elegant	Fairly Mature	Fine Bubbles	Peppery	Powerful

Finesse	Finish	Flabby	Fruit Forward	Tannin	Tart

Corky	Intense Flavors	Red Fruit	Up-front	Acidity	My Wine Shirt

MY
WINE ™
SHIRT

Hand Painted

GET A HAND PAINTED T-SHIRT;
WE USE *red wine* AS PAINT.

Learn more and see how My Wine Shirt started:
Guts-Ad.com/Wine

www.ingramcontent.com/pod-product-compliance
Lightning Source LLC
Chambersburg PA
CBHW031535040426
42445CB00010B/547